It's About Time

A step-by-step guide for understanding basic rhythms.

Designed for band, choirs, orchestras and private study.

by Ron Middlebrook
with Dick Sheridan

ISBN 978-1-57424-372-7
SAN 683-8022

Cover art by James Bennett | Jamesbennettart.com

Design by James Creative Group

Copyright © 2018 CENTERSTREAM Publishing
P.O. Box 17878 - Anaheim Hills, CA 92817

www.centerstream-usa.com | centerstrm@aol.com | 714-779-9390

A, A♯/B♭, B, C, C♯/D♭, D, D♯/E♭, E, F, F♯/G♭, G, G♯/A♭

At CENTERSTREAM Publishing we've got these arranged in ways that can make you cry, burn, shred, giggle, love, hate, explore, wonder, ponder, and understand. It's astonishing what those little notes can do.

In Dave Celentano's hands he shred them, Ken Perlman's banjo wound them into melodic songs, Joe Weidlich's mandolin twisted them into old patterns, Brian Emmel's bass slapped them in shape, John Klemmer's sax put them into classic songs, Glenn Weiser's harmonica blew them into old familiar patterns, Max Palermo's bass exercises made them the ultimate, Ron Middlebrook turned them into a best seller. David Brewster's guitar made them harmonize together and Dick Sheridan put them together to make his Ukulele say "Mahalo". Find out what these little notes have done for others and can do for you, send for your Centerstream catalog today.

P.O. Box 17878 - Anaheim Hills, CA 92817
(714) 779-9390   centerstrm@aol.com | www.centerstream-usa.com

Contents

"Centerstream has done it again with another great instructional music book. This time addressing the life blood of music – rhythm. It's about time someone wrote an easy to understand and well-paced book on rhythm and "It's About Time" by Ron Middlebrook does just that. Performing and reading music requires a mastery of rhythm and this book will help you develop that skill from the ground up."

David Hall
Band Director at Santa Fe Christian Schools

"Kudos to Ron Middlebrook for authoring a fun, simple and easy-to-understand book on teaching how to read and perform all the basics of rhythm and timing. The clever title, "It's About Time" and the eye-catching cover are sure to draw curious readers into buying the book."

Thornton Cline
Grammy and Dove Nominated
Centerstream Author, teacher and performer

"'It's About Time" an awesome book that finally focuses on teaching the beginning Music Student how to count! Why can't Music Students count? Because beginning method books combine reading pitches, producing notes on the instrument and counting simultaneously, which usually is too much at once. What doesn't happen using this approach? Counting! "It's About Time" is a must have book for teaching Music!

Pete Gamber
Private Music Lesson Teacher
Music inc Columnist "The Lesson Room"
NAMM University Speaker (Music Lessons)
Sabian Education Network Speaker

Chapter One

IT'S ABOUT TIME

Once upon a time ... time flies like an arrow ... Tempus Fugit ... just in time ... time was ... at the same time ... time on my hands ... no time to spare ... time to go ... time out ... in the nick of time ...

Our language is loaded with expressions about time, all linked to the tick of the clock. In music the meaning of time is related but somewhat different. It refers to how fast or slow the music is going -- called TEMPO -- and how that speed is divided into pulses and surges and is expressed in very specific ways.

Let's explore this musical world of time. But first we need to define several terms and concepts to build the necessary ground work for our journey.

To begin with, music has two main components: PITCH and RHYTHM. Pitch is the high and low of sound whereas rhythm is the duration of that sound, the long and the short of it, and its accents.

The Gershwin brothers, George and Ira, give a good example of it in the melody and lyrics of their 1930 song, "I Got Rhythm" -- "*I got rhythm, I got music ...*"

Rhythm is composed of BEATS. These are the pulses of sound, fast or slow, arranged in various patterns and phrases of duration and silence. Another composer, Cole Porter, incorporated it into his 1932 song "Night and Day":

> *Like the beat beat beat of the tom-tom ...*
> *Like the tick tick tick of the stately clock ...*
> *Like the drip drip drip of the raindrops ...*

NOTES are used to express pitch and the duration of sound. They are the symbols for putting the sound of music into written form. First we'll look at these notes and their time values. Later on we'll join them to pitch. To begin we need to examine two additional terms, MEASURE and TIME SIGNATURE.

The double bar line before the time signature indicates that the lines and spaces of the staff have no pitch. Notes entered on these lines and spaces have no pitch. They are just for rhythm and time value.

The Measure

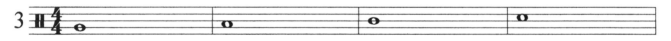

Measures (also called bars) are compartments separated by vertical lines called bar lines into which notes are placed. Each measure contains a certain number of beats which is consistent throughout a musical piece. The number of beats in a measure is determined by the time signature.

The Time Signature

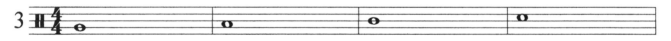

Notice in the example for THE MEASURE that there are two numbers one above the other in the first measure. This is the time signature. It occurs at the beginning of a piece. The top number 4 indicates how many beats there are in each measure. The bottom number 4 show what kind of a note gets one beat, in this case a QUARTER NOTE which will be explained later. Other time signatures might be 2/4, 3/4, 6/8, and there are others. Another name for the time signature is METER. Ocasionally the time signature can change within a composition. A symbol that looks like a backward letter C is often used for 4/4 time.

The Whole Note

Behold the WHOLE note. It looks like an empty cricle with no vertical line (stem) or "flags" attached to it. It is held for 4 beats. Instruments like horns or the violin can sustain (prolong) a sound; other instruments like the guitar or piano must sound the notes and then pause letting the sound linger for the duration of beats.

The Half Note

The shape of the HALF NOTE is an empty circle with a stem extending from it. Stems can go up or down and can be on either side of the notehead. The time value of the half note is 2 beats. In 4/4 time there would be two half notes for each measure.

The Quarter Note

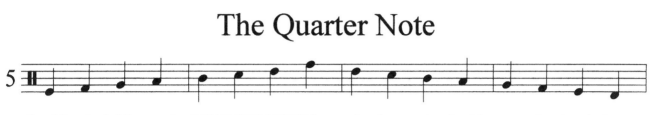

Just like the half note, the QUARTER NOTE has a circular notehead with a stem, but its circle is filled in and is solid black. Each quarter note gets 1 beat. In 4/4 time there would be 4 notes per measure.

The Eighth Note

Put a FLAG on a quarter note and you have an EIGHTH NOTE. It takes two of them to equal a quarter note and requires eight to fill a measure in 4/4 time. Eighth notes can be written separately or connected with heavy horizontal lines called BEAMS. Typically groups are in combinations of two and four with stems going either up or down.

The Sixteenth Note

The SIXTEENTH note has 2 flags and 16 of them would be required to fill a measure in 4/4 time. That's a lot of notes and usually only several of them are used in a measure combined with other notes to achieve the correct number of beats. Notice that in the progression of notes -- whole, half, quarter, eighth, sixteenth - each one has half the value of its predecessor. Connected sixteenth notes have double beams.

The Dot

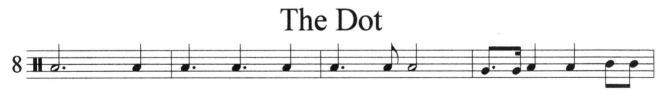

When a DOT is placed after a note it increases the time value of that note by half. A dotted half note, for example, gets three beats, two for the half note and one for the dot. A dotted qurarter note gets 1-1/2 beats, one for the quarter note and half a beat for the dot. The examples shown above are in 4/4 time. Each measure gets a total of four beats.

The Tie

The TIE is a curved line -- an arc-- that connects two notes of the same pitch. It extends the time of the first note by the value of the second note. In the first measure above, in 4/4 time, the half note is extended by the quarter note for a value of three beats. In the next measure the whole note has an added value of the quarter note, i.e. five beats. Observe how the tie crosses the bar line. The second note of the tie is NOT played. It just extends the value of the first note.

The Rest

Whole Rest   Half Rests   Quarter Rests

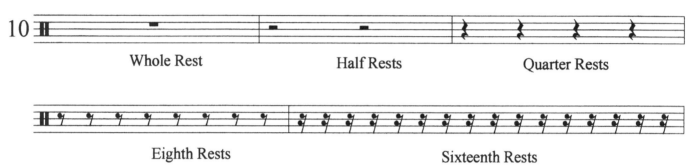

Eighth Rests   Sixteenth Rests

In music as in life, sometimes the sound of silence is golden. The rest marks a period of time in music where there is no sound. How long that silence is held for is determined by rests that have time values equivalent to notes. In the first measure above, the symbol -- like an inverted top hat -- is called a whole rest. In 4/4 time the silence is held for four beats. Turn that top hat right side up and it becomes a half rest worth two beats of silence. Two half rests would fill a measure in 4/4 time. What looks to some like a sea gull is the quarter rest worth one beat. The eighth rest like an eighth note has a flag and it's worth an eighth of a beat. Similarly, the sixteenth rest has two flags and its duration is one-sixteenth of a beat.

Here are some examples that combine notes and rests:

Here's a quick review of notes, rests, their shapes, and time values in 4/4 time.

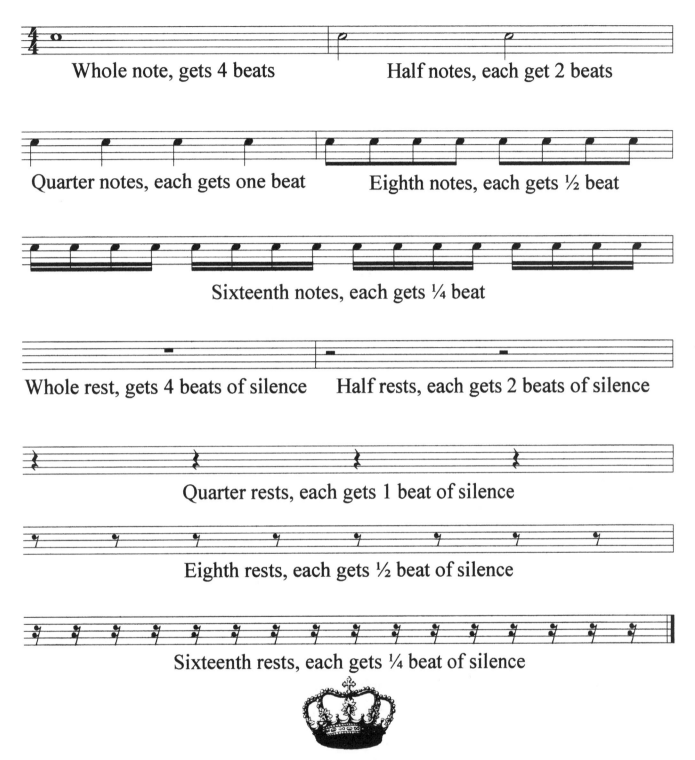

Whole note, gets 4 beats   Half notes, each get 2 beats

Quarter notes, each gets one beat   Eighth notes, each gets ½ beat

Sixteenth notes, each gets ¼ beat

Whole rest, gets 4 beats of silence   Half rests, each gets 2 beats of silence

Quarter rests, each gets 1 beat of silence

Eighth rests, each gets ½ beat of silence

Sixteenth rests, each gets ¼ beat of silence

English Queen Elizabeth the 1st (1533-1603) was the daughter of King Henry VIII and Anne Boleyn. Known as Good Queen Bess, Elizabeth was said to have commented: *"All my possessions for a moment of time."*

Chapter Two

Now that we've established the groundwork, let's roll up our musical sleeves and get to work. Using just C notes we'll explore some basic rhythm patterns for different time signatures, adding along the way some ties, rests, and dots. Those C notes are just for time values and not pitch. In the next chaper you'll find real notes to play.

Something useful to have is a METRONOME – one of those mechanical or digital electronic devices which click beats at various speeds.

Like a clock's pendulum, the weight on the swinging arm of a mechanical device can be moved up or down to control its speed. A graded scale behind the weight shows the speed in numbers and musical terms like *presto* (fast), *andante* (medium), and *largo* (slow).

Various metronome styles are available online, both digital and mechanical. Some have special features like instrument tuners and built-in rhythm patterns. There are even wearable devices that use vibration pulses instead of sound. Prices range from inexpensive to costly.

Let's assume you have a metronome. Set it for a moderate speed of say 100. For our purposes now each tick is a beat and will represent one quarter note. As you listen to the pendulum, try counting the beats. Accenting the "1" beat will help you keep time. Ready? Okay, here we go with different time signatures:

2/4 time: 1 2 1 2 1 2

3/4 time: 1 2 3 1 2 3 1 2 3

4/4 time: 1 2 3 4 1 2 3 4 1 2 3 4

6/8 time: (Count each 8th note as one beat)

1 2 3 4 5 6 1 2 3 4 5 6 1 2 3 4 5 6

As we practice notes and rhythms in the next chapter, different tempo speeds will be assigned, so keep your metronome handy.

All of the following examples are in 4/4 time -- 4 beats to the measure. Don't forget that the "C notes" on the staff are only designations for rhythm, not for pitch.

WHOLE NOTES and WHOLE RESTS

As we've seen in Chapter One, each whole note and whole rest gets 4 beats. The rest that looks like a top hat turned upside down can hold all 4 beats.

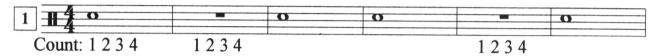

Count: 1 2 3 4   1 2 3 4   1 2 3 4

The numbers below each staff are to help you count the beats
The lage number at the beginning of a staff line (called a signature) is for quick reference

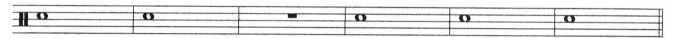

HALF NOTES and HALF RESTS

Reminder: For a half note we put a stem on the open circle of the whole note and give it 2 beats. The top hat of the half rest is turned right side up where it can only hold 2 beats.

QUARTER NOTES and QUARTER RESTS

Remember that quarter notes have a solid black note head. Their stems can go either up or down depending on their placement on the staff: notes below the middle line on the staff go up. Notes above the middle line go down. Notes on the middle line can go either up or down. Don't you agree that quarter rests have the appearance of a seagull?

11

Eighth notes can be written separately or connected with a beam in combinations of two, three, four, and eight notes. The eighth rest has the appearance of a miniature tomahawk.

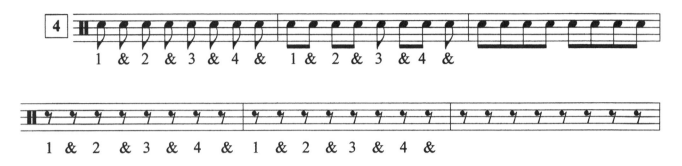

SIXTEENTH NOTES and SIXTEENTH RESTS

Characteristic of the sixteenth note is the double beam. The sixteenth rest has double tomahawks. Notes can be separate or beamed in various combinations with rests.

ADAPTING NOTES AND RESTS TO TIME SIGNATURES

So far we've been working with 4/4 rhythm. It's about time to branch out to other time signatures -- 2/4, 3/4/ 6/8 -- and even a little more in 4/4. We'll start with 2/4 time. It's sometimes referred to as "march time" because its beat of ONE-TWO / ONE -TWO is perfect for a marching cadence of LEFT-RIGHT / LEFT-RIGHT. Think of a military drill sergeant calling out:
"Lift 'em up and set 'em down. Put some rhythm on the ground."

Time Marches On

Musicians often speak of playing a "back beat" or "off beat." In 2/4 time the emphasis would be not on the first beat but the second, One-TWO / One-TWO.

2/4 TIME

Two-four time has the same quater note in the bottom of its time signature as does 4/4 time. The only difference is that in 2/4 time there are just two beats in each measure. The count is ONE-two, ONE-two, with the accent on the first beat. It's a great meter for marches and upbeat music. Jump on the computer and listen to the following musical examples. See if you can hear the 2-beat pulses: *Willaim Tell Overture*, Grieg's *Norwegian Dance* (included in Centerstream's *Classical Songs for the Ukulele)*, George M. Cohan's *You're A Grand Old Flag*, and don't forget *Yankee Doodle*.

Now for some complicated rhythms. Go slow. Hang on, Snoopy! You can do it!

Two "beets"
to the measure

PRELIMINARY RHYTHM PRACTICE
In 2/4 Time

3/4 Time

So far we've been looking at 2/4 time with 2 beats to a measure, also 4/4 time with 4 beats per measure. Now we'll check out 3/4 timing where each measure has three beats. This is sometimes referred to as "waltz time" or an Oom-Pah-Pah sound. To get those beats we'll use a combination of notes, dots and ties. Remember that with tied notes only the first note is sounded. Its time value is extended by the note it's tied to. Dots increase the value of a note by half.

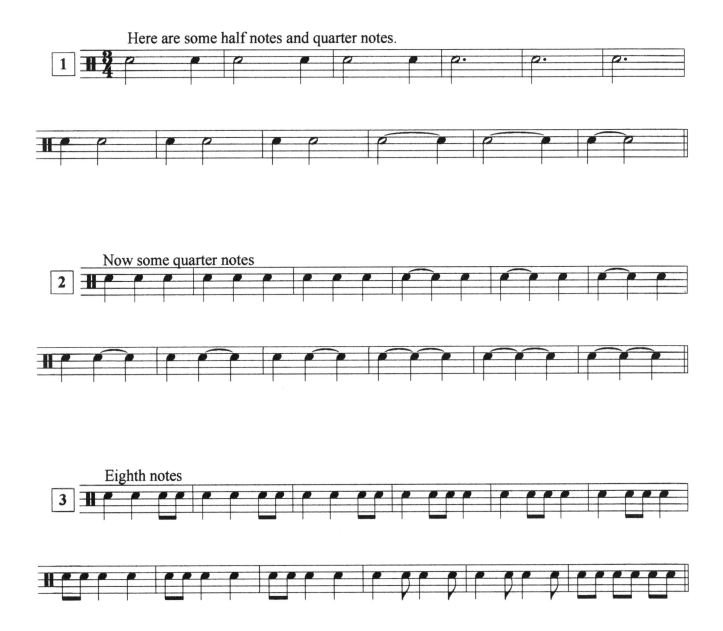

15

Sixteenth notes

Mix and match

Oom Pah Pah

PRELIMINARY RHYTHM PRACTICE

In 3/4 Time

4/4 TIME

So far we've seen 4/4 time in various forms, using it to explore the time value of notes, rests, ties and dots. With a more focused look, let's put all of these elements together with a few additional examples and some preliminay rhythm practice. Don't forget that the C-notes are only for rhythm and not for pitch. In the third chapter we'll play real notes in true pitch, utilizing all of the time values we've been working on. Here we go in 4/4 time: 4 beats to the measure with each quarter note getting one beat.

PRELIMINARY RHYTHM PRACTICE
In 4/4 Time

6/8 TIME

Six-eight time can fool you. Sometimes it sounds like a waltz and at other times like a rollicking Irish jig. Of course by now we can see that it consists of 6 beats to the measure and each 8th note gets one of those beats. Count: 1 2 3 4 5 6 for each measure. Take a look at the following three examples from Centerstream's *Yuletide Favorites for Ukulele*.

PICKUP MEASURES: You'll notice that some of the following songs start off with notes that don't total up to a full measure. These introductory notes are called pickups and give you a running start into the song.

How about these additional examples from Centerstream's *Irish Songs for Ukulele*.

In 6/8 time eighth notes get 1 beat, quarter notes get 2 beats, half notes get 4 beats. Dotted quarter notes get 3 beats, while a dotted half note gets 3 beats. Remember: it takes two sixteenth notes to equal an eighth note.

PRELIMINARY RHYTHM PRACTICE
In 6/8 Time

This sign means to repeat the previous measure.

Repeat previous measure

THE TRIPLET

The triplet is typically a group of three 8th notes packed together and played as if they had a time value of only two of those 8th notes. Whoa! What does that mean? In 4/4 time those two 8th notes equal the time value of a quarter note. So we could say that the triplet compresses three notes into one beat. Tricky, huh. The count is the beat number (1-2-3-4) followed by "and-a". If the triplet falls on the first beat we'd count it as "1-and -uh" or "2-and-uh" if it falls on the second beat, and so on. The three eighth notes of our triplet are joined together by a beam or sometimes by a bracket or curved arc placed above or below the triplet with a number 3 superimposed. The word count of a triplet can also be "trip-el- it," but this lacks the beat count number.

Here are some examples:

Try counting using numbers: 1 2 3 4 5 6. Don't forget that the tripled eighth notes get 2 beats.

Time flies like an arrow. Fruit flies like a banana.

Rhytn Rhythms

Can you write the counts of each note and rest below?
The first line (and tips in each line) is done for you.

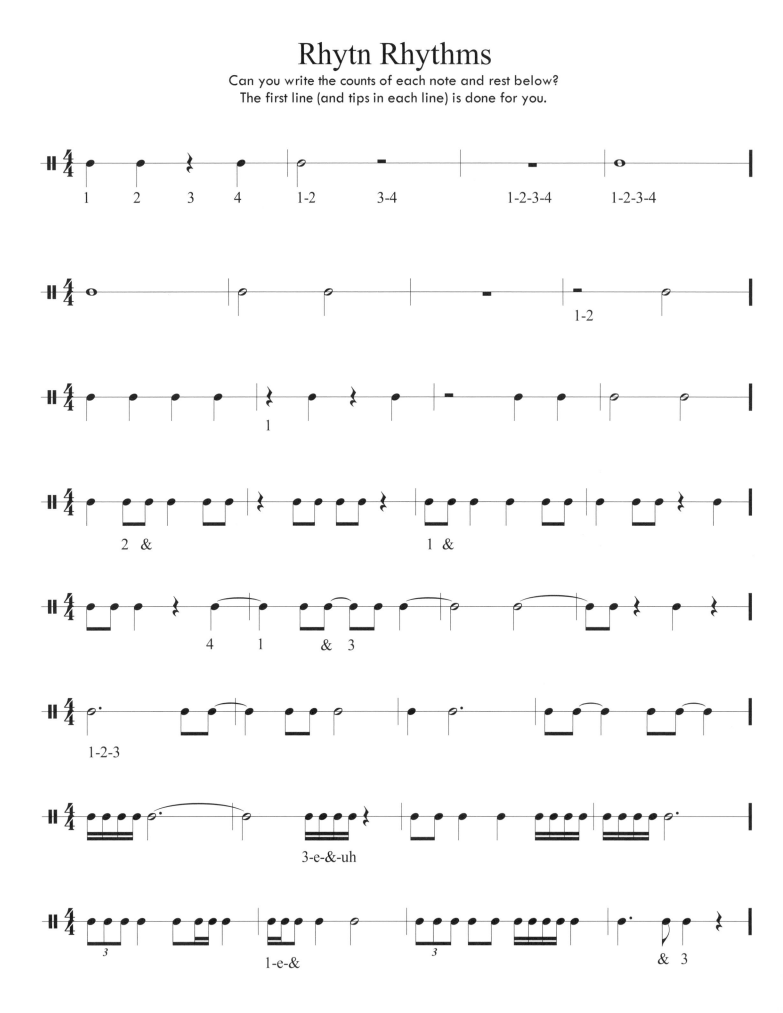

CHAPTER 3

In this chapter we'll take a closer look at the different time signatures we've already explored. We'll add many more examples of each. In addition we'll introduce tempo, that is the speed at which practice examples should be played. Tempo indications will range from slow to fast. But here's something else that's new: now, instead of using just "C" notes to indicate time values, we'll place real notes on the staff. So besides rhythm we can hear pitch.

Remember how in Chapter 2 we introduced the metronome, that device digital or mechanical which sets the speed of music. Our examples in this chapter will have both metronome numbers and words. With numbers we can specify exact speed. Words, however, only suggest tempo. Since they are not exact they give a degree of latitude to the performer allowing interpretation. The words most often used come from the Italian. Here are some of them: *Lento = slow (40 to 60 beats per minute), Largo = also slow (40 to 60 bpm), Adagio = at a walking speed (76 to 108), Moderato = moderate (108 to 120), Allegro = fast (120-168), Presto = very fast (120 +).*

Symphonic conductors can set the speed at which the orchestra will play a piece. Sometimes their interpretations are quite controversial, pacing the tempo much faster or slower than what might be expected.

It's interesting to note how some of these tempo terms are sometimes used in the title of compositions, like Samuel Barber's haunting *Adagio for Strings* and *Largo* (also known as *Going Home*) from Dvorak's *New World Symphony.* Let's not forget the magician who with a wave of his hand and a cry of *Presto!* pulls a rabit from his hat.

One New York City Hospital considers tempo so important that it maintains a playlist of songs for use in cardiac chest compression (CPR) ranging in beats from 100 to 120 per minute.

In the following practice exercises there'll be some bits and snatches of well known songs. See if you can recognize them. Try playing them at different speeds. Experiment!

PRACTICE EXERCISES IN 2/4 TIME

With Note Pitch and Tempo

PRACTICE EXERCISES IN 3/4 TIME
With Note Pitch and Tempo

PRACTICE EXERCISE IN 4/4 TIME
With Note Pitch and Tempo

PRACTICE EXERCISES IN 6/8 TIME
With Note Pitch and Tempo

Andante - Walking pace (88 beats per minute)

Moderate (120 bpm)

Presto - fast (170)

Chapter Four
♥ Love at First Sight
Sight Reading

It's about time we put all our hard work to the test. For the remainder of this book, let's use what we've learned so far with some "sight reading" song exercises. Before we turn the page take a look at the following:

Sight Reading is the ability to take a piece of music you've never seen before and play it in time and with the correct notes and expression. For a professional musician it's obviously a valuable skill, but for the rest of us -- for instrumentalists of all abilities -- it's a doorway that can open new worlds of musical fun and enjoyment.

To be a good sight reader you'll need to know (1) the notes on the staff, (2) where those notes are on your instrument, and (3) and to understand time notation -- and, of course, that's what this book has all been about.

Now it's time to get started with the tips below:

1. **Practice:** Since sight reading is a skill like any other, day-to-day repetition will improve your ability. Even a few minutes spent at the end of each practice session will reap rewards. Begin with less difficult work and each day increase the challenge.

2. **The Metronome:** The best aid to discipline is the metronome. It substitutes for playing with other musicians and serves as a constant reminder of the forward movement of music. It also reins in the tendency to rush and pushes you rhythmically. If a passage is too difficult, slow down the beat, then repeat it gradually increasing the tempo setting. Train yourself to pay attention to the metronome. Your tempo may vary slower or faster from day to day. This is to be expected.

3. **Scan the Page:** Don't dive head first into a new composition. Look before you leap. You have many things to consider. Take your time as you carefully scan the printed page. Separate any new material to be learned from that which you already know. Next, look for the fastest moving notes, and imagine how they'll fit into the tempo indication. Spot which passages seem awkward.

4. **Key Signature:** Look at the key signature before you play a single note. Remember what key you're in and if any key changes are in the music.

5. **Time Signature:** Apply the above recomendations to time signatures. Be careful not to play the wrong number of beats in a bar.

6. **Repeats:** Are there any? Where does the repeat go back to? On your own, learn the meaning of D.S. (del segno), D.C. (da capo), and Coda. Don't get lost in the music.

7. **Scales, Patterns, and Arpeggios:** Look for these to see if they are repeated. They'll help you save some brain waves when reading.

8. **Don't Stop:** Once you begin to sight read a passage, don't stop. Keep going, no matter how tangled up you might become. Keep your eye moving across the page at the tempo of the music. Don't look back at the mistake you might just have made, and don't leap too far forward. But do keep your eye just aheadof the notes you are playing; as you increase your experience you'll find it easier to read ahead. Try to grasp an entire measure in one glance without changing your focal point. Many good sight readers acknowledge that one of the keys to good sight reading is looking a bar ahead.

9. **Mistakes:** You'll make mistakes sight reading. Let them go by. No matter what your level of experience, don't panic. Try to anticipate what the next musical gesture will be, and try to enjoy the experience. The proper attitude for sight reading is alert interest. Look upon sight reading as an adventure that will bring satisfaction and a sense of accomplishment.

Remember that any rhythm, no matter how complex, is really no harder than a combination of quarter and half notes. Don't confuse difficulty in reading with difficulty in playing. They are separate. Analysis and memory are the keys to good sight reading. They are the two main elements of the complete musician.

SAMPLE SONGS
In 2/4 Time
Put On Your Old Grey Bonnet

STANLEY MURPHY

PERCY WENRICH

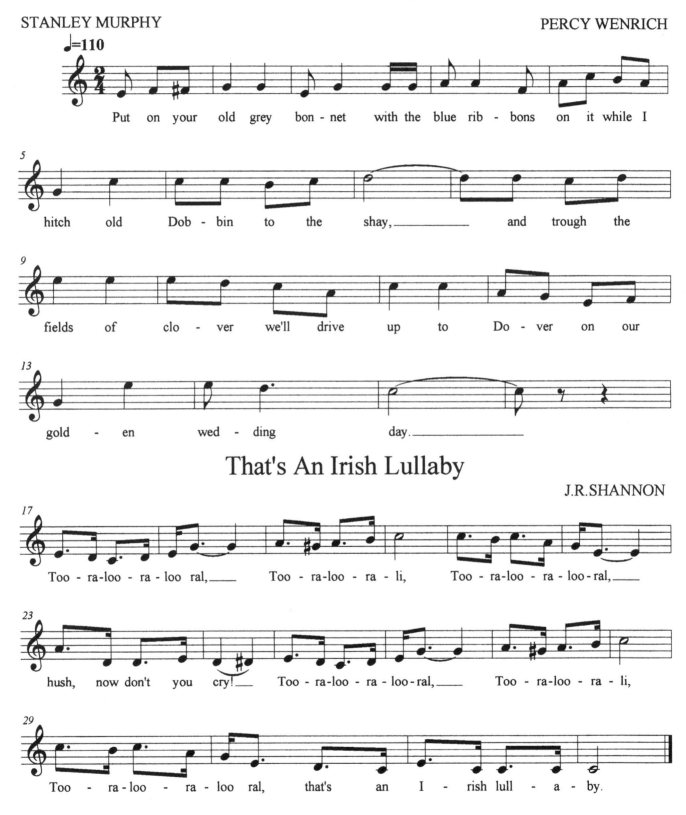

That's An Irish Lullaby

J.R.SHANNON

SAMPLE SONG

In 3/4 Time

When Irish Eyes Are Smiling

CHAUNCEY OLCOTT and GEORGE GRAFF, JR.   ERNEST R. BALL

SAMPLE SONG
In 4/4 Time
America The Beautiful

KATHERINE LEE BATES

SAMUEL A. WARD

The time signature for 4/4 time can also be indicated by a C, called "common" time. A vertical line drawn through the C is called "cut time." Its time signature is 2/2, two beats to the measure, each half note getting one beat.

ADDITIONAL SAMPLE SONG
In 4/4 Time
Raymond

AMBROISE THOMAS

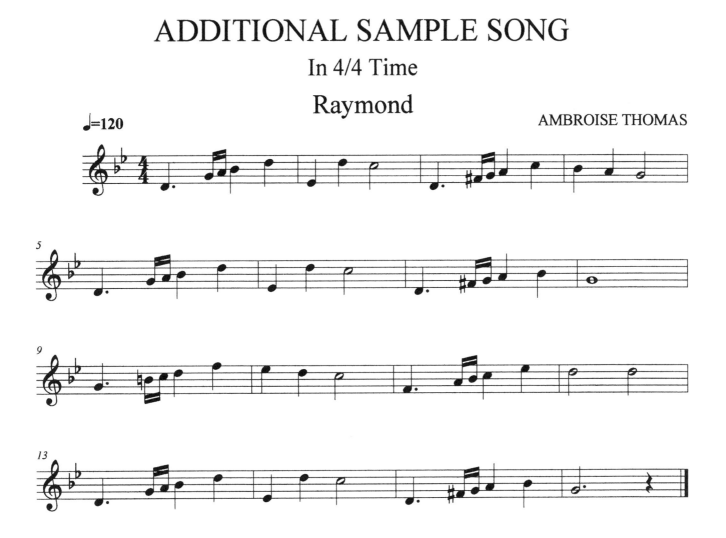

This lively piece from the overture to the French opera of the same name is a selection from Centerstream's *CLASSICAL MUSIC for the UKULELE*. The book includes more that 40 of the world's most beauiful and enduring light classic masterpieces.

SAMPLE SONG
IN 6/8 TIME
Home On The Range

BREWSTER M. HIGLEY

DANIEL E. KELLEY

Oh, give me a home where the buf - fa - lo roam, where the deer and the an - te - lope play,_____ where sel - dom is heard a dis - cour - ag - ing word, and the skies are not cloud - y all day._____

Home, home on the range,_____ where the deer and the an - te - lope play,_____ where sel - dom is heard a dis - cour - ag - ing word, and the skies are not cloud - y all day._____

SAMPLE SONG
In 4/4 Time
William Tell Overture

GIOACCHINO ROSSINI

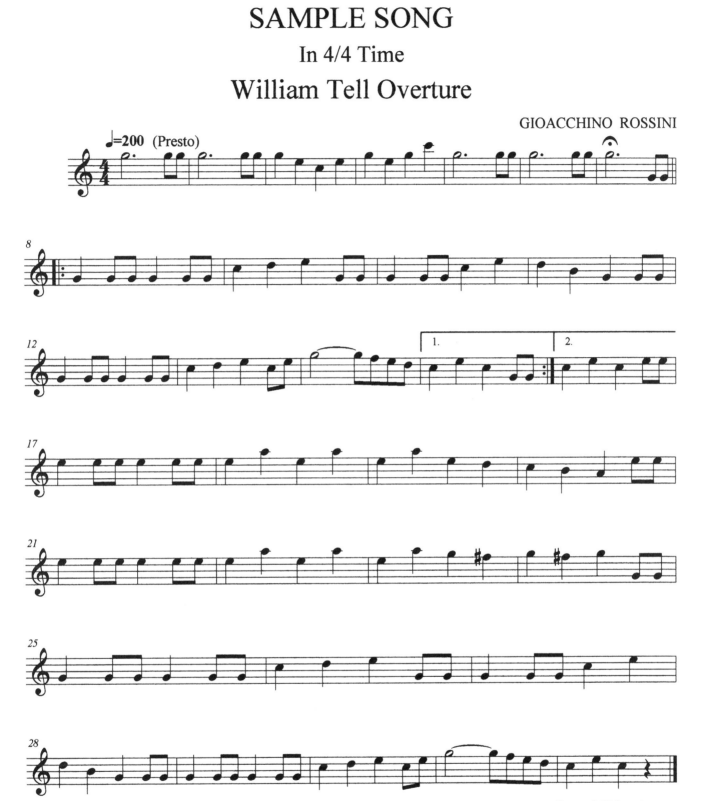

This familiar overture from the opera *William Tell* was the theme for the Lone Ranger radio and TV series.
"From out of the past come the thundering hoofbeats of the great horse Silver! Hi-Yo, Silver!"
The Lone Ranger rides again!

IT'S ABOUT TIME
~A conclusion~

Timing is everything, whether in music, business affairs, sports, or simply being on time for an important meeting, a class, or personal engagement. What would happen to the stand-up comedian, the juggler, or the"man on the flying trapeze" if their timing were off? Pity the poor dancer with "two left feet who doesn't heed Yankee Doodle's caution to "mind the music and the step." Few drummers are in demand if it is said they rush the beat or drag it down. Telegraphers and ham radio operators once had to learn Morse Code with its sequence of short dots and long dashes. Classical poetry has both rhyme and rhythm. It's all about time.

And what wisdom is contained in the saying that a stitch in time saves nine. How many disasters could be avoided by heeding that simple proverb.

The story is told of a band leader talking to a vocalist saying, "We'll start your song in 3/4 time, then speed up to a fast 4/4, finally slowing down to a march tempo in 2/4 or 6/8. Let's change the key every couple of measures."

"How do you expect me to do all that?" the vocalist asked.

"You had no problem doing it that way last night," the frustrated band leader replied.

Obviously the vocalist's timing and sense of pitch was off. It happens. But not with the careful student who's mastered the guidelines of this book.

Yes, it's all about time. We've learned how to determine note values and understand time signatures. We've practiced sample songs and exercises to sharpen our skills. We've come a long way, and now it's time to put to use what we've learned and worked so hard to acquire.

There comes a time to conclude, to say our time is up. And so we leave you, but not before wishing you the unending joys of music and the very best of times.

SYMBOLS AND TERMS

ACCENT – TO EMPHASIZE A NOTE.

AL FINE – ("AL FEE-NAY") PLAY TO THE END.

ALLA BREVE – "CUT-TIME." HALF NOTES RECEIVE ONE BEAT.

ARPEGGIO – THE NOTES WITHIN A CHORD (USUALLY NOTES 1, 3, AND 5 IN A SCALE).

CHROMATIC – USING HALF-STEPS IN BETWEEN NOTE NAMES (EX. F#). A SCALE USES ALL OF THEM.

CODA – "THE TAIL," OR A SPECIAL ENDING.

COMMON TIME – 4/4 TIME. QUARTER NOTES RECEIVE ONE BEAT.

CRESCENDO – TO GRADUALLY GET LOUDER.

CUT TIME – "ALLA BREVE." HALF NOTES RECEIVE ONE BEAT.

DA CAPO (D.C.) – THE BEGINNING. OFTEN FOUND WITH "AL FINE" (TO THE END).

DAL SEGNO (D.S.) – "THE SIGN." OFTEN FOUND WITH "AL FINE" (TO THE END) OR "AL CODA."

DECRESCENDO – TO GRADUALLY GET SOFTER. SEEN WITH SEVERAL NOTES, UNLIKE ACCENTS.

ENHARMONICS – TWO NOTES THAT SOUND THE SAME WITH DIFFERENT NAMES (EX. C# AND Db).

FERMATA – HOLD A NOTE UNTIL YOUR INSTRUCTOR INDICATES A RELEASE.

FINE – THE END.

FORTE (f) – LOUDLY.

FORTISSIMO (ff) – VERY LOUDLY.

MARCATO – A SHORT ACCENT.

MEZZO FORTE (mf) – SOMEWHAT LOUDLY.

MEZZO PIANO (mp) – SOMEWHAT SOFTLY.

MODERATO – A MEDIUM TEMPO.

OCTAVE – DISTANCE BETWEEN TWO NOTES WITH THE SAME NAME (THE BOTTOM AND TOP OF A SCALE).

PIANO (p) – SOFTLY.

RITARDANDO (rit.) – TO GRADUALLY SLOW DOWN.

SLUR – A CURVED LINE INDICATING TO NOT TONGUE TWO OR MORE DIFFERENT CONNECTED NOTES.

STACCATO – TO PLAY A NOTE SHORT.

SYNCOPATION – A STYLE OF RHYTHM THAT NATURALLY EMPHASIZES NOTES ON "AND" COUNTS.

TEMPO – THE SPEED OF THE MUSIC.

TENUTO – TO PLAY A NOTE TO ITS FULL LENGTH.

TIE – A CURVED LINE INDICATING TO NOT TONGUE TWO OR MORE OF THE SAME CONNECTED NOTES.